BRITAIN SINCE 1930

Leisure Time

Philip Sauvain

WAYLAND

BRITAIN SINCE 1930

The Advance of Technology
Leisure Time
Life at Home
Life at Work

Cover pictures: (Above) A happy crowd of employees at Charing Cross Station about to leave for their annual outing in Margate in 1935, (below left) a family enjoying leisure time in the 1990s, (below right) a child listening to a stereo in the 1990s.
Title page: A railway poster from 1932.
Contents page: An American jukebox from the 1940s.

Series editor: Francesca Motisi
Series designer: Joyce Chester
Production controller: Carol Titchener

First published in 1996 by
Wayland (Publishers) Ltd
61, Western Road, Hove
East Sussex BN3 1JD, England

British Library Cataloguing in Publication Data
Sauvain, Philip
Leisure Time. – (Britain since 1930 Series)
I. Title II. Series
790.0941

ISBN 0-7502-1652-2

Printed and bound by B.P.C. Paulton Books, Great Britain

Picture acknowledgements
The publishers would like to thank the following for allowing their pictures to be reproduced in this book: British Airways 22 (below), Hulton Deutsch *cover*, 20; Joel Finler 13; John Frost Collection 5 (above); Francesca Motisi 29 (below); The Robert Opie Collection *contents page*, 17; Philip Sauvain 4, 5 (above/right), 5 (below), 6 (both), 7 (both), 8, 9, 10 (all), 11, 12, 14 (both), 15, 19 (below), 21 (both), 22 (above), 25 (both), 26 (both), 27 (both), 29 (above); Science Museum/Science & Society Picture Library – LNER poster Scarborough by Austin Cooper *title page*, 24; Topham Picturepoint 16, 18, 19 (above), 23, 28.

Contents

Home entertainment

Since 1930, more and more workers began to enjoy the benefits of a shorter working day and a shorter working week. It gave them more free time to spend at home. At the same time, higher wages and the availability of cheap, labour-saving devices gave people the opportunity and the time for leisure pursuits such as home entertainments, hobbies, games and sports, day trips and holidays.

Men leaving Dockyard, Unicorn Gate, Portsmouth

78619.

⇦ A picture postcard showing workers leaving the dockyard in Portsmouth. Sixty or seventy years ago, most people worked much longer hours than workers do today. Factory and office workers worked on Saturday mornings as well as during the week.

In 1930 the pattern of family entertainment was changing. Many people preferred to stay in at night to listen to the radio instead of going out to the pub.

By 1939 there were over 11 million wireless sets in Britain. Radio became even more popular during the Second World War. The blackout and the risk of air raids meant that most people stayed at home at night. The radio helped to keep up their spirits with entertainment programmes, such as *Garrison Theatre*, *Workers' Playtime*, and the twice-a-day, non-stop programme *Music While You Work*.

THE **CHRISTMAS NUMBER**

RADIO TIMES

"JUST A SONG AT TWILIGHT"

6D.

NATIONAL PROGRAMMES

NAT. (1,500 Metres), LON. NAT. (261.1 Metres), NORTH NAT. (296.2 Metres), WEST NAT. (261.1 Metres), SCOT. NAT. (285.7 Metres).

10.10.—NATIONAL only—Daily Service.
10.30.—NATIONAL only—Time, weather.
10.45.—Cooking for Children, by Mrs. K. Dent.
11.0.—Reginald New (organ).
11.30.—For Schools: Music and Movement for Very Young Children. Except
    SCOTTISH—Excerpts from Scott's Waverley Novels.
11.50.—New Victoria Cinema Orchestra, Clarry Wilson (piano).
12.30.—B.B.C. Dance Orchestra.
1.15.—Friday Midday Concert.
2.0.—Time; For Schools: Date Groves in Iraq. Except
    SCOTTISH—Scottish Studio Orchestra (until 3.15).
2.30.—Music lesson (except SCOTTISH).
3.0.—Friday Afternoon Story, by Frank Roscoe (except SCOTTISH).
3.15.—To Unemployed Clubs.
3.35.—East Anglian Herring Fishing Bulletin.
3.40.—B.B.C. Northern Orchestra.
4.30.—Hotel Metropole Orchestra.
5.15.—Mantovani and his Tipica Orchestra.
6.0.—Time, news, weather, special notices.
6.30.—Keyboard Talk: Beethoven, by D. F. Tovey.
6.50.—In Your Garden, by C H. Middleton.
7.10.—From Plainsong to Purcell; Foundations of English Music; Wireless Singers.
7.30.—Kentucky Minstrels; with Scott and Whaley, Percy Parsons, Ike Hatch, C. Denier Warren; Kentucky Banjo Team: Joe Morley, Tarrant Bailey, Jnr., Dick Pepper; Harry S. Pepper and Doris Arnold at the pianos; B.B.C. Theatre Orchestra and Male Voice Chorus, conducted by Leslie Woodgate.
8.30.—News Out of Scotland: programme for St. Andrew's Day.
9.30.—Time, news, weather.
10.0.—Causes of War—8, by Major C. H. Douglas.
10.15.—B.B.C. Orchestra (section D).
11.10.—Reading: Mary Morison, What can a Young Lassie Do Wi' an Auld Man? and A Red Red Rose, by Robert Burns, read by Alistair Sim.
11.15-12.0.—NATIONAL only—Harry Roy and his Band.

Many people took an interest in hobbies at home in the 1930s, 1940s and 1950s, such as woodwork, model-making, dressmaking and stamp collecting. Collecting cigarette cards was another popular hobby at a time when many people smoked. Each packet of cigarettes had a picture card inside forming part of a set of pictures. Children swapped cards to make up complete sets and stuck them in the albums provided by the manufacturers.

⇧ You can see what type of radio programme people listened to in the 1930s from the 'All-In Radio Timetable', published in *The Daily Mirror* for Friday, 30 November 1934. As you can see, there were no disc jockeys then.

HOBBIES 1952
1/6 HANDBOOK

WITH FREE DESIGN

⇦ A *Hobbies Handbook* from 1952.

⇧ Dressmaking designs in the magazine *Home Notes* in September 1939.

There were magazines and comics for all the family (see below), such as *Passing Show* (April 1936), *Sunbeam* (December 1939) and *Woman* (December 1947). Illustrated news magazines like *The Sphere*, *Picture Post*, *Illustrated* and *Everybody's* kept people up to date with the latest news. ⇩

More people stayed on at school and many more people could read. Libraries flourished and the cheap tabloid newspapers increased their sales. They offered readers free gifts and set prize competitions as well as printing football pools coupons and a daily crossword.

Teenagers and young people had less reason to stay in at home – as a former Teddy Boy recalled in a BBC interview. Teddy Boys were so called because they wore similar fashions to those worn in the Edwardian period, which was named after King Edward (Teddy) VII.

Boredom in the late 1940s by a Teddy Boy

'Every night out, you know. There wasn't any home entertainments like television. Sunday nights you had nothing else to do but walk around Newcastle, looking in shop windows, parading yourself again in your regular outfits.'

TELEVISION

Burl Ives
the famous American folk-singer with his young son Alexander. He pays a return visit to television at 9.45.

3.15 ABOUT THE HOME
Practical help for the housewife
Presented by Joan Gilbert
Frances Perry describes the work to be done in the flower and vegetable beds

Garden Furniture
A selection from the exhibition recently arranged by the Council of Industrial Design

Ants
Bill Dalton explains how to keep ants out of the house

Bees
Reginald Gamble offers further advice to new bee-keepers
Edited and produced by S. E. Reynolds

4.0-4.15 **WATCH WITH MOTHER**
For the very young

Andy Pandy
Maria Bird brings Andy to play with your small children and invites them to join in songs and games
Audrey Atterbury and Molly Gibson pull the strings
Gladys Whitred sings the songs
Script, music, and settings by Maria Bird
(A BBC Television film)

* * *

5.0-5.35 **CHILDREN'S TELEVISION**
John Wright's Marionettes
Mr. Bumble introduces a programme of puppet antics, including Joey the Clown and his Catapulting Chair, and Achmudt the Sinister Sand Dancer
Assistant Operators, Jane Tyson and Joan Garrick

Children's Newsreel

Cal McCord
the popular cowboy with 'Ladybird'

7.0 Maureen Pryor, John Gregson
Rachel Gurney, Betty Cooper in
'THE PASSIONATE PILGRIM'
A television play
by Michael Barry
and Charles Terrot
from Charles Terrot's novel
'Miss Nightingale's Ladies'
(Second performance: for details see Sunday at 8.40)

8.55 Interlude

9.0 NEWSREEL

9.15 BASKET BALL
Harlem Globe Trotters
v.
American All Stars
from the Empire Pool
and Sports Arena, Wembley
The warming-up and part of the game between two of America's leading teams over here on a European tour
Commentator, Patrick Burns

9.45 BURL IVES
with his guitar

10.0 DOWN YOU GO!
with Roy Rich
laying the clues
and
Elizabeth Gray
Kenneth Horne
Paul Jennings
and Helen Shingler
finding the letters
Special effects by Alfred Wurmser
The game devised by
Polly S. and Louis G. Cowan
Presented by Brian Tesler

10.30 app. Weather Forecast and
NEWS (sound only)

NEXT WEEK
'ALL ON A SUMMER'S DAY,' a play by R. F. Delderfield (Sunday)

THE PASSING SHOW: 'ALL OUR YESTERDAYS' (Monday)

YEHUDI MENUHIN (Monday)

THE COURSE OF JUSTICE: Magistrate's Court (Tuesday)

VISITS to the Royal Tournament (Wednesday and Friday)

TROOPING THE COLOUR (Thursday)

THE FIRST TEST MATCH at Nottingham (Thursday to Saturday)

Jewel and Warriss in RE-TURN IT UP! (Saturday)

Television made little impact before 1950, even though it had been first demonstrated as long ago as 1927. It became popular, however, after the televising of the Queen's Coronation in 1953. Suddenly, everyone wanted a TV set.

From about 1955 onwards, watching television became Britain's main leisure interest. Instead of going to the cinema, people ate TV dinners on a tray in front of their set. Neighbours complained about people staring at the TV screen instead of joining in a conversation. Children said they could not do their homework because the television was on. Television even became the main topic of conversation at work the next day.

Watching television in about 1957. Notice the small size of the screen, not much bigger than the clock on the sideboard. People re-arranged their furniture so that everyone could get a good view of the television screen. ⇩

⇧ Television programmes listed in *The Radio Times* for Thursday, 4 June 1953. Notice how there is only one channel and how programmes began at 3.15 in the afternoon and ended at 10.30 pm.

Music hall, theatre and cinema

In the years before television, most towns of any size had a theatre or a music hall and several cinemas. Theatres with the same company of actors put on different plays each week, while music halls and variety theatres, like London's Palladium, put on a twice-nightly show of popular singers, dancers and comedians, such as Sir Harry Lauder, George Robey, Max Miller and Marie Lloyd.

Live theatre shows faced two main challenges – from the cinema in the 1930s and from television in the 1950s. Many theatres had to close or were turned into bingo halls. Variety shows disappeared but despite all the competition, live theatre survived and is still flourishing in many parts of Britain. A number of completely new theatres were built in the 1970s and 1980s to cater for new audiences keen to see a live show instead of a film or television programme.

PALLADIUM
London, 1 October 1938
Twice nightly at 6.15 pm and 9.00 pm

Nervo and Knox;
Naughton and Gold;
Flanagan and Allen;
Sue Ryan
(impressionistic comedienne);
Stuart Morgan Dancers;
Badminton champions;
De Tuscans (world-famous fencers);
Fanica Luca;
Princess Kuulei etc.

Many big spectacles –
galaxy of International Stars.

⇧ Advertised in the *Daily Herald*, 1 October 1938.

⇦ London theatre programmes from the mid-1950s. London's theatres were then (and still are) a big tourist attraction and continued to flourish despite competition from television and the cinema.

In 1930, the cinema was the newest and most exciting form of entertainment a town could offer. The old silent films had been replaced by the talkies and many new cinemas were being built.

The first talkies

1929: 'I had often been taken to the cinema to see silent films. However, to Newcastle came the first "All Talking, All Singing and All Dancing" film – **The Singing Fool** *with Al Jolson. My parents took me to Newcastle to see this film, and we had to wait for a long time in a queue outside the Stoll Theatre. How bitter was my disappointment when I discovered that I couldn't understand a word that the actors were saying [because of their American accents]. On top of that, the harsh and raucous voices frightened me.'*

With their imposing appearance, uniformed commissionaires outside, long queues of people waiting to go in, smart, uniformed usherettes and ice-cream girls, cinemas were a big attraction. Heavy plush curtains surrounded the screen and a cinema organist on a platform rose up out of the bowels of the cinema to entertain the audience. This was a relic of the old silent films when a pianist played appropriate music to accompany the moving pictures on screen.

"Hats and the Man" by Maurice Chevalier

JANET GAYNOR

FREE INSIDE
Beautiful Art Plate in Full Colours of

FRANCES DEE and JOEL McCREA

⇐ Magazines (shown left), such as *Film Weekly* (27 December 1930) and *Film Pictorial* (26 February 1938), were very popular with film fans.

Many imposing new cinemas were built in the 1930s, such as the Majestic cinema at King's Lynn in Norfolk, seen here in 1977. ⇩

The attractions of the cinema were greatly increased in 1935 when *Becky Sharp*, the first feature film in full colour was shown.

Colour starts new era for films

10 July 1935: 'Yesterday I saw film history made. Becky Sharp *is the greatest sensation since* The Jazz Singer *and* The Singing Fool, *brilliantly photographed in colours that will hit the public right in the eye – sky blue, brilliant yellow, dazzling scarlet.'*

⇦ Film stars of the 1930s depicted on cigarette cards.

Cinemas were closed when war broke out in September 1939, but soon reopened. They played a vital role in the war, giving everyone the chance to forget their worries for a time. Wartime audiences expected performances to be interrupted by air raids. Customers could get their money back if they wanted but many stayed to see the film. *'Few moved, I can tell you,'* said one Londoner. *'Who cared if a bomb did drop. One would go out happy.'*

Notice in a Wartime cinema

'If an air raid warning be received during the performance the audience will be informed. Those desiring to leave the theatre may do so.'

⇐ A leaflet listing forthcoming attractions at the Odeon Cinema, Bury-St-Edmunds, not long after the start of the Second World War in December 1939. The picture itself shows the Odeon in London's Leicester Square.

Wartime visit to a cinema in 1941

'We took our gas masks in case of an air raid. The cinema was near the town hall in the square where they held "War-Weeks" to raise money for the war effort. We saw The Marx Brothers Go West. *I can see the cinema now. It was small and gloomy – probably because there were no lights outside because of the blackout.'*

After the war, some cinemas began to close down as more and more people stayed at home to watch television instead of going out for their entertainment.

This is why the big film companies tried out new ideas to meet the challenge of television. Since the television screen was very small and only showed pictures in black and white (at that time), with very poor sound from a single loudspeaker, cinemas went in the other direction. Spectacular new movies, such as *The Robe* and *The Knights of the Round Table* were filmed in rich colours with stereophonic sound. They were projected on to massive new widescreens, using processes such as CinemaScope, Cinerama and Panavision. Despite this, cinema attendances continued to fall.

Special 3-D (three-dimensional) movies were also filmed. They had to be viewed through special cardboard spectacles to get the feeling that you were watching a three-dimensional live performance.

A poster for the spectacular CinemaScope movie *Ben Hur* shown in 1959. ⇩

Going to a 3-D film in 1953

'It was weird! You were given a pair of these cardboard spectacles as you went in. The films were full of gimmicks. They set up the scenes to make the most of the 3-D effect. People walked between pillars and objects were thrown at the camera to make you duck. As a craze it only lasted a year or two. The only good 3-D film I saw was the musical Kiss me Kate *starring* Howard Keel *but I've seen it since on television and it's just as good in two dimensions as it was in three.'*

Despite gloomy forecasts in the 1950s and 1960s by people who thought the cinema was doomed, it survived. However, cinema attendances today are only a tenth of what they were forty years ago. In the 1970s and 1980s most large cinemas were subdivided into separate rooms so that several films could be shown on different screens at the same time.

Rock and pop

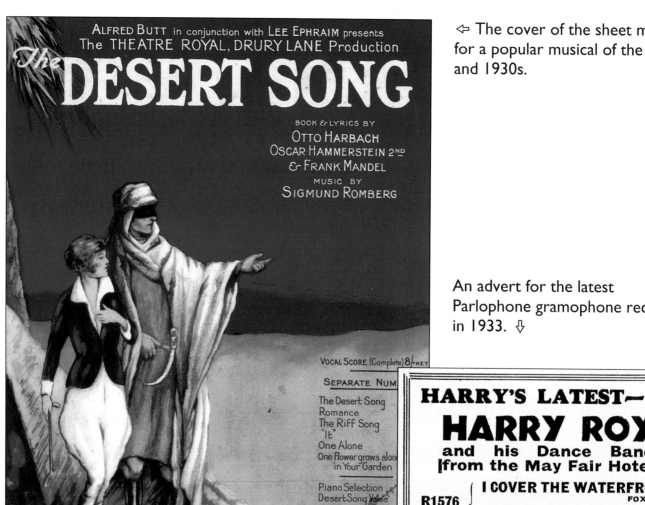

⇐ The cover of the sheet music for a popular musical of the 1920s and 1930s.

An advert for the latest Parlophone gramophone records in 1933. ⇓

Much of the popular (pop) music of the 1930s, 1940s and 1950s was played by dance bands with about ten to twenty musicians, such as the bands led by Ambrose, Roy Fox, Ray Noble, Henry Hall and Lew Stone. Singers with the band, like Al Bowly, were called crooners. You could hear their music every night on the radio and during the day.

⇦ An advert for a radiogram in 1937. They were very expensive. A farmworker would have had to work for seven months to earn the money to buy this one.

The popular hit numbers of the day could be heard on records. These were about the same size as a modern record but thicker, heavier and made of brittle, black plastic. If you dropped one, it broke. Young people usually played them on portable wind-up gramophones. You had to wind the motor up by hand every time you played a record. Each side only lasted about three minutes and the heavy steel needle, which was used to play the record, often stuck in the groove and could wear out the surface. The records were called 78s because they spun round on the turntable of the gramaphone at a speed of 78 rpm (revolutions per minute).

⇦ Dancing at the Palais or Locarno in 1954.

Dancing was a popular pastime during the war and afterwards. In the 1950s and 1960s, most large towns had a Palais, Mecca or Locarno ballroom.

Dancing at the Locarno in 1963

'I can see them now – the Locarno, Wakefield, and the Locarno, Bradford – with their illuminated signs and dancers queuing outside. You always got impatient as you neared the door since you could hear snatches of music inside as people went in. Sometimes it was so packed, you couldn't dance properly at all. You just clung to your partner and moved when the crowd moved. They stamped your hand if you wanted to go out, so you could come back in again.'

In the 1950s record manufacturers brought out a much smaller disc to replace the old 78s. Instead of hard plastic, it was made of soft, unbreakable vinyl and rotated slowly at speeds of 33 1/3 or 45 rpm. As a result, the playing time of these LP (Long Playing) and EP (Extended Play) records was much greater than that of the 78s they began to replace. They were followed in 1958 by the first stereo LPs, in the 1970s by small audiocassettes, and in the 1980s by thin metal compact discs using laser beams to play back the sound.

The most popular hits in the hit parade could be heard on radio – as a former National Serviceman recalled when remembering his days in the RAF in the early 1950s.

The hit parade in 1952

'I used to get back to camp on Sunday evenings some time after half past eleven. All the lights were on in the barracks and as I walked in, the loudspeaker would be blaring out the latest hits at Number 11 or Number 12 on the Radio Luxembourg Top Twenty.'

Meanwhile the type of music that teenagers had danced to in the 1930s and 1940s had changed. The first major change came when dancers began to jive or jitterbug instead of dancing face-to-face. By the end of the 1950s, rock'n'roll was all the rage.

The first American jukeboxes were seen in Britain in about 1947. All the latest hits could be played at the drop of a coin. ⇨

⇦ Police hold back fans of Bill Haley, the pioneer of rock'n'roll on his arrival in London in 1957.

Rock around the clock in 1956

'Police were called to five cinemas to deal with excited young people creating disturbances during showings of the film Rock Around the Clock. *The film is based on jive music. Teddy boys and girls started by clapping hands and banging their feet to the rhythm of the music. As the tempo grew faster they left their seats to dance in the gangways.'*

A few years later the British rock bands of the 1960s were popular throughout the world, headed by the Beatles, Rolling Stones and other pop groups. For the first time, the ideas, music and clothes of young people had become news.

⇦ Gerry and the Pacemakers performing in the Cavern Club in Liverpool in 1964. Scores of rock groups, such as Freddie and the Dreamers and The Kinks became household names in the 1960s, after appearing on television programmes such as *Top of the Pops*.

Beatlemania

7 July, 1964: 'Beatlemania reached a new height in Piccadilly Circus last night. More than 10,000 teenagers, many of them screaming, surrounded the London Pavilion to see the Beatles arrive for the premiere of their first film,* A Hard Day's Night. *The noise was almost frightening. Ambulance men had to fight their way through the swaying mass to bring out women and girls who had fainted.'*

Radio and television played a big part in promoting rock music through the broadcasts of disc jockeys and popular television programmes like *Top of the Pops*. It led to the rapid decline of the big bands and the old-style ballroom dancing. Their place had been taken by the gramophone record, the discotheque and the disc jockey.

Magazines like *Valentine*, *Record Mirror* and *New Musical Express* became the modern equivalents of the film fan magazines of the 1930s. ⇨

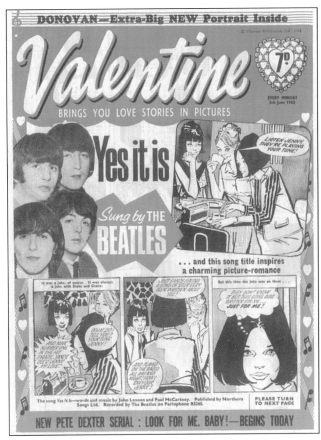

Sports and games

In the 1930s and 1940s road traffic was still relatively light and motor cars were still something of a rarity in some country districts. As a result, children expected to be able to play in the streets. *'No cars on the road,'* recalled a Norfolk woman, *'so one could have great fun whipping a top or skipping to school.'* In school playgrounds, children's games followed a set pattern throughout the year.

Children's games in the early 1940s

'There was the conker season in the autumn, of course, and sliding and snowballs in winter, but there were also other seasonal games such as flicking cigarette cards and bowling hoops, playing marbles and spinning tops in the spring when the weather was warmer. The girls played skipping games, chanting the same rhymes each time. They also played hopscotch in the streets after chalking out squares on the pavement.'

⇦ Children playing in the street in the 1940s.

⇐ New sports such as greyhound racing, speedway and motor racing became popular during the 1920s and 1930s.

Adult interest in sports and games in the 1930s was very limited compared with the wide interests people have today. The *Daily Express* had news items about fourteen sports on Monday, 6 October 1930, compared with thirty-two sports mentioned in the *Daily Telegraph* on Monday, 27 March 1995. Soccer and rugby were the main interest then in winter and cricket and tennis in the summer. Many people were only interested in the sports they could bet on, such as football pools and illegal street betting on horse racing.

⇑ West Ham captain George Kay (left) shakes hands with Bolton Wanderer's captain Joe Smith (right) before the start of the 1923 FA Cup Final. Notice the long shorts worn by the players. The official attendance at the game was 127,000 – a record. But police estimated that somewhere between 200,000 and 300,000 spectators – 'the biggest football crowd ever assembled' – actually saw the game after a huge number of people broke through the barriers. It was a miracle no one was killed.

⇐ Headlines in the *Sunday Pictorial*, 29 April 1923.

WEMBLEY STADIUM STORMED BY EXCITED CUP FINAL CROWDS

CUP FINAL CHAOS THAT WAS NEARLY A DISASTER

STADIUM GATES STORMED BY 100,000 PEOPLE

Broken limbs and serious injuries in great rush and struggle with the police.

Many women crushed.

Pandemonium at stations.

⇦ Lawn tennis in 1934. Men still played in long trousers and women in long skirts.

At Wimbledon in July 1934 Britons had a double reason to cheer. Fred Perry became the first and only Englishman to win the Men's Singles at Wimbledon since 1909, and Dorothy Round won the Ladies' Singles Final.

Between 1939 and 1945 most sporting competitions were cancelled for the duration of the Second World War. However, teams representing the armed services played against teams from abroad, such as the Royal Australian Air Force cricket team.

Sport in Britain was revived after the war, boosted by the first post-war Olympic Games held in London in 1948. ⇨

After 1960 many more young people began to enjoy taking part in individual sports rather than team games. Climbing, skiing, badminton, golf, yachting, skateboarding, lawn tennis, table tennis, cycling, athletics, snooker, swimming, hang gliding, roller disco, windsurfing and many other sports and games have made it possible for almost everyone to find a sporting activity they actually enjoy. Children at school took part in a much wider selection of sports and games than their parents or grandparents did.

Television has since played a big part in enabling people to enjoy sports they would not ordinarily have taken an interest in, such as baseball and American football. There is also a much greater emphasis on keeping fit today.

⇦ One of the most outstanding post-war sporting achievements was the England World Cup win in 1966.

Holidays

Going to the seaside for a week's holiday became a national habit in the 1930s, 1940s and early 1950s. These were the years that brought prosperity to Britain's seaside resorts. It was a time when millions of people, especially those in the Midlands and South-East, felt better off. They could afford to go away for a few days to the sea. Visitors left on packed excursion trains to join the thousands jam-packed on crowded beaches and piers at the coast.

August Bank Holiday in 1926

'Southend had a tidal wave of visitors which swamped hotels and boarding houses. By six or seven o'clock on Sunday night not a room was to be had anywhere. Night found at least 10,000 people sleeping on the beach and cliffs. There were bathers in the sea at all hours. All shelters were occupied, Others slept beneath boats, at the side of breakwaters, under bathing huts, refreshment kiosks and the pier. The number of people sleeping out was easily a record. For over six miles there was one line of sleepers. The wonderful weather brought out thousands of road vehicles everywhere, while trains to the sea could not carry another passenger.'

⇧ A railway poster encouraging people to travel to Scarborough in 1932.

Bathing costumes in 1934. ⇩

⇧ Holidaymakers enjoying a ride in a charabanc (an open-topped, single decker bus) at Rhyll in North Wales in the late 1920s.

Blackpool in 1933

'Compared with this huge mad place, with its miles and miles of promenades, its three piers, its gigantic dance halls, its variety shows, its switch-backs and helter-skelters; its army of pierrots, bandsmen, clowns, fortune-tellers, animal trainers; its seventy special trains a day; places like Brighton and Margate and Yarmouth are merely playing at being popular seaside resorts.'

In some northern towns all the mills and factories closed down at the same time for the town's Wakes Week to enable families to go away. Many went to the same seaside resorts. Barnsley went to Bridlington, Bradford to Morecambe and Stoke-on-Trent to Llandudno in North Wales.

This is an extract from a holiday diary written by a Blackburn teacher on holiday on the Isle-of-Man in 1936. ⇩

Motorists, cyclists and hikers enjoyed a different type of holiday in the 1920s and 1930s, using large-scale maps like this to explore the British countryside. ⇩

G R

ORDNANCE SURVEY
Tourist Map
DUNOON AND
THE CLYDE
Scale: 1 Inch *to* 1 Mile.

PRICE
Three Shillings

A holiday in the Isle of Man. 1936

Tuesday July 21st Chara trip round the Island — Douglas, Laxey, Ramsey Peel, Tynwald Hill, Rushen Abbey.

Sat July 25th Went to Douglas to see Marie off. Rained all the time we were in Douglas. The Lady of Mann was in harbour. Such crowds, we never thought the ship would accommodate all, but it did & sailed away at 4-10 (10 mins late)

Friday Aug. 14th
Our last day & what a morning, wild & wet What a prospect for crossing in the Lady of Mann.
Written on board.
Here we are rolling about a bit on the ocean. Edith has gone to lie down a bit & Mother is keeping her company in the ladies' room. Alan is running about enjoying the pitching motion whilst up to now (½ hr from Fleetwood)

Your older relatives may be able to tell you about their holidays in the 1930s. Some may even have a holiday diary like the one shown opposite.

Barbed wire blocked access to many beaches during the Second World War because it was feared they might be used by enemy landing craft. Concrete pill boxes and guns defended cliff-tops. Piers were closed and guarded by troops. But after the end of the war, the holiday resorts soon revived. They were helped by a new law – the Holidays with Pay Act in 1938 – which gave eleven million workers the right to holidays with pay. Now many more people could afford to go away. Billy Butlin advertised cheap, all-inclusive holidays at the seaside. They were an instant success.

⇧ A postcard of the Victoria Pier, Douglas, Isle-of-Man – posted on 11 August 1937.

Butlin's Holiday Camp in 1946

'The normal day at Butlin's begins at 7.45 when the camp radio gives a hearty rise-and-shine call to the camp. "Good morning, campers. It is a lovely day and the sun is shining (or, the weather has let us down) so show a leg you lads and lasses, rub the sleep out of your eyes and prepare for another grand day of fun, another Butlin's jolliday."

The campers go back to work thoroughly refreshed. The weary mother has had her children well-cared for in the nursery, the lonely have been partnered in a dance or at tennis, the pale have been well-fed and caught the sun.'

A Butlin's holiday camp advert in *Illustrated* magazine, February 1952. ⇨

27

After 1960, however, Britain's seaside resorts had to meet a new challenge. Cheap air travel made it possible for people to travel much further afield. Tour operators and travel agents sold cheap package holidays abroad, mainly to the new resorts which were rapidly developing along Spain's *costas* – her hot, dry and sunny Mediterranean coasts. People in Britain who enjoyed higher wages and longer periods of holidays with pay could now afford to spend a week or a fortnight abroad – often for little more than the cost of a similar holiday in Blackpool or Yarmouth. As air travel became even cheaper and as living standards continued to rise, holidaymakers went even further afield. By 1995 it was no longer unusual for people in ordinary jobs to go skiing in the Alps in winter or take their annual summer holiday in California, Australia, Africa or the Far East.

⇐ An advert for holidays in Spain published in *The Illustrated London News* on 29 September 1951. Notice how the advert features hotels and places in Spain's cities and countryside. The magnificent Mediterranean beaches are not even mentioned!

Modern holiday brochures for Spain attract millions of tourists each year to Spanish seaside resorts like Benidorm (shown here) and Torremolinos further along the coast. ⇨

Glossary

Beatlemania The name used in the 1960s to describe the screaming, over-excited fans when they became hysterical, at the sight or sound, of a rock group such as The Beatles.

Charabanc An open-topped, single decker bus which was used to take day-trippers on excursions in the 1920s and 1930s.

Cigarette card A picture card in a pack of cigarettes which was one of a set, such as famous film stars.

CinemaScope The widescreen process first used in 1953 in *The Robe.*

Cinerama Widescreen process of the early 1950s which used three projectors running at once to produce a huge panoramic screen giving audiences the impression of actually being in the centre of the action on screen, such as on a roller coaster ride.

Crooner A singer with a dance band in the 1930s and 1940s.

Excursion train A special train taking passengers to a particular place, such as a seaside resort, for a cheap day out.

Holidays with Pay Act The law passed by Parliament in 1938 which gave workers the right to annual holidays with pay. In the past, many workers had to do without wages when they took a holiday.

Jitterbug (see jiving) .

Jiving The jerky American dance of the 1940s which was performed to music with a strong beat.

Jukebox A large automatic gramophone in a café or pub which had a number of the latest hit records, any one of which could be played at the press of a button when you inserted a coin.

Labour-saving device A machine which reduces the amount of human effort needed to do a job, such as a dishwasher in the kitchen.

Laser An extremely narrow beam of light which is so accurate it can be used to read the microscopic signals on a compact disc.

Music hall A theatre with a small orchestra which put on twice-nightly variety shows of singers, dancers, acrobats, magicians and comedians. You could usually get a meal and a drink there as well.

Package holiday An all-inclusive holiday organized by a tour company and paid for in advance.

Panavision A similar widescreen process to CinemaScope.

Radiogram A combined radio and gramophone in a wooden cabinet which played back sound through a large loudspeaker.

78s Thick, breakable, black plastic records which rotated on a gramophone turntable at a speed of 78 rpm (revolutions per minute).

Silent film A film made before the coming of the talkies in the late 1920s. Subtitles told the audience what was happening on screen and a pianist in the cinema played music appropriate to the scene on screen, such as a lively march when soldiers were shown.

Teddy Boys Youths in the 1950s and early 1960s who wore long sideburns, slicked-back greasy hair, extra-long jackets with velvet collars and tight drainpipe trousers. They were often involved in trouble with the police.

Variety show (see music hall).

Wakes Week The period of the summer when all the mills and factories in some northern towns closed down for the week to enable families to go away together to the seaside.

Wind-up gramophone A portable gramophone on which records were played using the handle at the side to wind up the motor which turned the turntable.

Books to read

Changing Times: The Seaside by Ruth Thomson (Franklin Watts 1992)

Changing Times: Toys and Games by Ruth Thomson (Franklin Watts 1992)

Exploring Sport and Recreation by Cliff Lines (Wayland 1988)

How They Lived: A Teenager in the Sixties by Miriam Moss (Wayland 1987)

How We Used To Live, 1954–1970 by Freda Kelsall (A & C Black 1987)

Looking Back: Family Life by Jennifer Lines (Wayland 1991)

Looking Back: Holidays and Pastimes by Philip Sauvain (Wayland 1991)

Timelines: Entertainment by David Salariya (Franklin Watts 1993)

Timelines: Sport by David Salariya (Franklin Watts 1993)

Twenty Names in Films by N Hunter (Wayland 1990)

Twenty Names in Pop Music by Andrew Langley (Wayland 1990)

Twenty Names in Sport by Toni Williamson (Wayland 1991)

Acknowledgements
Grateful acknowledgement is given for permission to reprint copyright material:
Page 6 From BBC Archive disc *Teddy Boys*, transcribed in *The Long March of Everyman*, edited by Theo Barker, Andre Deutsch and the BBC, 1975
Page 9 Slightly abridged from *British Cinemas and their Audiences* by J.P. Mayer, Dennis Dobson, 1948
Page 10 By Campbell Dixon in *The Daily Telegraph*, 10 July, 1935
Page 12 From an interview conducted in 1993
Page 16 From an interview in 1990
Page 18 From *The Daily Telegraph*, 8 September 1956
Page 19 From *The Daily Telegraph, 1964*
Page 24 Report in *The Daily Mirror*, 3 August 1926
Page 25 From *English Journey*, by J.B. Priestley, Heinemann, 1934
Page 27 Extract printed in *Life in a Holiday Camp*, Picture Post, 13 July 1946.
While every effort has been made to trace copyright holders, the publishers apologize for any inadvertent omissions.

Index

Numbers in **bold** refer to illustrations